What is a Key Word?

A Key Word is a common word that children must learn on sight. They are the building blocks of reading because they appear so often. School reading schemes are based on Key Words so whatever scheme your child uses at school, these books will support it, they will also reinforce his/her reading, learning and develop his/her reading confidence and fluency.

Although Key Words are so common they are not always easy to learn. Most children find it much harder to remember 'the' than 'apple'. One of the reasons for this is that mentally they can make a picture of an apple, but they cannot make a mental picture for 'the'. Your child will need lots of encouragement.

What is an Incidental Word?

Other words, which are not Key Words, are introduced in the stories. This has been done to develop the second of the reading skills, that is, 'context'. The idea is that your child should try to guess the word by a) looking at the picture, b) thinking of a word which would make sense in the context of the sentence and story, and c) looking at the first letter of the word and thinking of a word that makes sense and starts with the right sound. Your child does not need to remember incidental words.

Attempting to read unknown words is very important. It is essential that you give your child lots of praise for a sensible guess. Never criticise an attempt, however wild. If the guess is wrong, supply the correct word, while praising the attempt.

Create a Feeling of Success

Your child must feel a sense of achievement for everything he/she reads. No matter how simple you think it is, give masses of praise. Young children need to feel that things are easy for them. If your child finds reading difficult, proceed very gently; find something which is easy so that he/she can develop a sense of success. Then you can pile on the praise and he/she will want to do more. Above all, don't push at this early stage. Keep it light-hearted and fun.

How to Use This Book

1. Write down the *Key Words* and show them to your child. Discuss the shape of the word, how many letters, what letter each starts with, etc. Write the words on separate cards and see if your child can learn one or two before starting the book. Find a page where a particular word appears and ask your child to point to the word.
2. If your child is quite confident, he/she might be happy to read straightaway. Otherwise, read the story aloud to your child first, pointing to each word as you do so. Spend time talking about the pictures because a great deal of the story is told in the pictures.
3. Ask questions, such as, 'What do you think will happen next?' Or 'Why did she do that?'
4. When your child starts to read the book, be very patient and encouraging. Never let him/her struggle over a word. Tell him/her what the word is.
5. Once you have reached the end of the book, encourage your child to read it as often as possible. One reading is not enough to learn the *Key Words*.
6. Use any of the activities suggested on page 28.
7. The text is specially designed to be read by a child who only knows the *Key Words* taught in this reading series. For this reason, you should start with the books in Level One and progress in order.
8. Avoid pressure and stress at all costs. Reading is fun.

Key Words introduced in this book:

wants a have says she play we now You very Now

Incidental Words:

busy Jenny biscuit drink story football tired video doctors

age 4-6

Key Words
readers
At home with Dad

Written by Nicola Morgan MA
an experienced teacher with a diploma in literacy teaching
Illustrations by Sara Silcock

Give lots of praise for reading, and stick the gold star reward sticker at the bottom of each right-hand page.

Key Words are printed in the coloured band at the foot of the page for the parent's reference.

Series editor: Nina Filipek
Series designer: Paul Dronsfield
Copyright © 1999 Egmont World Limited.
All rights reserved.
Published in Great Britain in 1999 by
Egmont World Limited, Deanway Technology Centre,
Wilmslow Road, Handforth, Cheshire SK9 3FB.
Printed in Germany.
ISBN 0 7498 4098 6

Dad is busy.

Jenny wants a biscuit.

wants a

Dad is busy.

Jenny wants a drink.

Can I have a story? Jenny says.

No, says Dad.
I am busy.

have   says

Jenny wants to play.
Can you play? she says.

No, says Dad.
I am busy.

play   she

Can we play now? she says.

You can see I am busy,
says Dad.

we now You
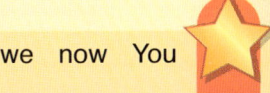

Can we play football?
she says.

Dad is very tired.

very

Can I have a video?
says Jenny.

You can have a video,
says Dad.

Jenny is tired.

Dad is very very tired.

Jenny wants to play.

Can we play doctors?
she says.

Now Dad wants to play!

Can I play? says Dad.

Now Mum is here.

Oh Dad! says Sam.

Reading is not just identifying the words in a story. To be an effective reader, and to enjoy reading, your child needs to understand, appreciate and respond to a story in different ways.

Here are some useful activities for you to do with your child. The activities will help iron out any difficulties and will extend your child's enjoyment and appreciation of the story.

It is vital that all reading activities are fun, so do give plenty of praise; never push your child too much or work when he/she is tired, cross or hungry.

Reading skills: take each of the key words introduced so far (and any other words which your child happens to know) and write them on separate pieces of card. Use the cards to make a simple sentence for your child to read. If your child knows the words well, you could make up some silly sentences. If not, choose one or two problem words and make sentences using them; expect your child to recognise only words which have been taught. Give lots of praise.

Writing: help your child make a story book. Your child can suggest all the words, you can do the writing and between you you can draw the pictures. This makes another simple reading book for your child's collection. (Note: remember to make the cover of the book, with the title, picture and author's name on the front.)

Story-telling: cover up the words in *At Home With Dad* and ask your child to tell the story in his/her own words. You may find that your child tells the story in a 'reading' voice, rather than normal speech: this is good, as it means that he/she has grasped the patterns of language used in story books.

Link to other areas of the curriculum: art: help your child make a sign for his/her bedroom door. Cut a circle from card; draw lines to divide it into 3 sections; write 'I am busy', 'I am sleeping' and 'I am playing' on the sections; make a cardboard arrow and fix it to the middle with a split pin.

5 Great **GIFTS**
to choose from

In many of the new Egmont World books you will find a special token. It is on the following page in this book. Start collecting the tokens to make massive savings on this exclusive range of products.

1

£5.99 RSP
only £3.99 (+p&p)
with 5 tokens

The stationery set, packed in a plastic carrying case, comes complete with many items, including a pencil case and set squares.

2

£5.99 RSP
only £3.99 (+p&p)
with 5 tokens

The teaching clock has special hands that move just like a real clock.

3

£3.99 RSP
only £1.99 (+p&p)
with 5 tokens

The pencil case has an integral calculator.

4 **5**

99p RSP **FREE** with 2 tokens
Choose either the alphabet or the times tables poster.

If you have any difficulty finding the other books in this series please contact Egmont World Ltd. on 01625 650011

SAVE UP TO £2 OFF Exclusive Gifts

Data protection: Personal data given by you on this form may be used to send you information about other special offers from Egmont World Ltd.

If you do not wish to receive such offers or services please tick this box.

ONE TOKEN

Simply decide which gift you would like and collect the correct number of tokens. The more you collect the more money you can save.

		one token	two tokens	three tokens	four tokens	five tokens	
1	stationery case	£5.99 ☐	£5.49 ☐	£4.99 ☐	£4.49 ☐	£3.99 ☐	MAXIMUM 5 TOKENS
2	teaching clock	£5.99 ☐	£5.49 ☐	£4.99 ☐	£4.49 ☐	£3.99 ☐	
3	calculator pencil case	£3.99 ☐	£3.49 ☐	£2.99 ☐	£2.49 ☐	£1.99 ☐	
4	alphabet poster	£0.49 ☐	FREE ☐				MAXIMUM 2 TOKENS
5	times tables poster	£0.49 ☐	FREE ☐				

Please tick the offer you require above. You may also use the tokens available in other Egmont World books.

Please complete the following details:

I enclose a cheque made payable to Egmont World Limited for £_____ (inc. p+p) Please send me the gift(s) I have indicated.

Name _____

Age _____

Address _____

_____

_____

Postcode _____

Title of this book purchased

_____

Where it was purchased

_____

Offer open to residents of UK, Channel Isles and Ireland only. Please allow 14 days for delivery. Egmont World Ltd. withholds the right to withdraw the offer. Offer subject to availability.

Please return this completed form together with your tokens and a cheque or p.o. to:
Activity Centre Offers, Egmont World Limited, PO Box 7, Manchester M19 2HD

Special Token

Please tape a £1 coin below to cover part post and packing costs.

£1

PLEASE STICK TOKENS BELOW

| Place first token here | save 50p | save 50p | save 50p | save 50p |

Once you have collected the required number of tokens, stick them to the spaces provided here and complete the form above.